D1105623

BOXER AND BRANDON

박서와 브랜든

www.kidkiddos.com

Copyright©2015 by S. A. Publishing ©2017 by KidKiddos Books Ltd.

support@kidkiddos.com

First edition, 2017

Translated from English by Tay Bake

영한 옮김 백태은

Korean editing by Jiwon Ahn

번역 감수 안지원

Library and Archives Canada Cataloguing in Publication Data

Boxer and Brandon (Korean Bilingual Edition)

ISBN: 978-1-5259-0438-7 paperback

ISBN: 978-1-5259-0439-4 hardcover

ISBN: 978-1-5259-0437-0 eBook

KidKiddos Books

Inna Nusinsky
저자 이나 누진스키

Illustrations by Gillian Tolentino
그림 길리안 톨렌티노

Hello, my name is Boxer. I'm a boxer. I'm a type of dog called a boxer. Nice to meet you! This is the story of how I got my new family.

안녕, 내 이름은 박서야. 난 박서 종이지. 개를 구분하는 종류 중 하나야. 만나서 반가워! 이 이야기는 내가 새로운 가족을 만나게 된 사연이야.

It all started when I was two years old.
내가 두 살 때 일이었어.

I was homeless. I lived on the street and ate out of garbage cans. People got pretty mad at me when I knocked over their trash cans.
난 집이 없었어. 거리에서 자며 쓰레기통을 뒤지며 살았지. 내가 쓰레기통을 넘어뜨리는 걸 사람들은 무척이나 싫어 했어.

"Get out of here!" they would shout. Sometimes I had to run away really fast!
"저리 썩 가지 못해!" 그들은 나에게 소리치곤 했지. 가끔은 엄청 빨리 달아나야만 했었어!

Living in the city can be hard.
도시에서 사는 건 때때로 고단했어.

When I wasn't looking for food, I liked to sit and watch people walk by on the sidewalk.
음식을 찾을 때가 아니면, 자리에 앉아 사람들이 지나가는 걸 구경하곤 했지.

Sometimes, I would look at people with my sad eyes and they would give me food.
가끔은, 내가 슬픈 눈을 하고 있으면 음식을 주는 사람들도 있었어.

"Oh, what a cute doggy! Here, have a snack," they would say.
"어머, 귀여운 강아지네! 자, 이거 먹어," 이렇게 말하면서 말야.

One day, a little boy and his dad were walking toward me.
하루는, 한 소년과 아빠가 내 쪽으로 걸어왔어.

"How's that sandwich, Brandon?" asked the boy's dad.
"샌드위치 맛있니, 브랜든?" 아이의 아빠가 물었지.

The sandwich
looked really good!
그 샌드위치는 정말 맛있어
보였어!

I put on my sad eyes.
The boy stopped and
held out his sandwich.
I was just about
to take a bite,
when...

나는 슬픈 눈을 하고 있었지.
아이가 멈추더니 나에게
샌드위치를 내미는 거야.
내가 얼른 한 입 먹으려는
순간…

"Brandon, don't feed that dog! He'll just come looking for more," exclaimed his dad. Brandon pulled the sandwich back.

"브랜든, 강아지한테 그런 걸 주면 안돼! 나중에 또 달라고 한단 말이야," 그의 아빠가 말했어. 브랜든은 샌드위치를 다시 가져갔지.

So close—I could smell the butter! Parents never want to share with me!

먹을 수 있었는데—버터 냄새가 정말 좋았는데! 부모들은 도통 나에게 뭘 주려 하지 않았지!

I whined as pitifully as I could as they walked away.

나는 슬프게 흐느끼며 그들의 뒷모습을 바라보았어.

After that, I decided to take a nap. I was having a wonderful dream.

그 후에, 낮잠을 자기로 했지. 너무 황홀한 꿈을 꾸었어.

I was in a park and everything was made from meat! The trees were steaks! It was the best dream ever.

공원에 있었는데 모든 게 다 고기인 거야!
나무는 스테이크였고! 그건 정말 최고의
꿈이었어.

Something woke me up, though. Right in front of me was a piece of a sandwich! I jumped to my feet and gobbled it down.

그런데 누군가 나를 깨웠어. 일어나보니 샌드위치 한 조각이 눈 앞에 있지 뭐야! 난 벌떡 일어나 허겁지겁 먹기 시작했지.

Mmmmm! It was so good! Just like my dream.

냠냠! 너무 맛있었어! 꿈 속에서 그랬던 것처럼 말야.

"Shhh," said Brandon. "Don't tell Dad." *What a nice little boy*, I thought to myself.

"쉿," 브랜든이 말했어. "아빠한텐 말하지마." 정말 착한 아이군, 난 생각했지.

Day after day, Brandon would come visit me and give me a snack. Then, one day...

날이면 날마다, 브랜든은 먹을걸 가져다 주었어. 그러던, 어느날…

"Hurry up, Brandon. You'll be late for school," said Brandon's dad.

"서둘러, 브랜든. 학교에 늦겠다," 브랜든의 아빠가 말했어.

"I'm coming!" shouted Brandon as he ran past, dropping a brown bag on the sidewalk.

"지금 갈게요!" 브랜든이 달려가며 소리쳤어, 갈색 봉지를 인도에 떨어트리면서 말이야.

Sniffing around, I walked up to it and looked inside. It was full of food!

코를 큼큼거리면서, 그게 무엇인지 보러 갔어. 안엔 음식이 한가득 있었지!

I was just about to eat it all when I thought of something. *Brandon always brings me food when I'm hungry. If I eat his food, then he'll be hungry.*

한 입에 다 먹어치우려는 순간 갑자기 어떤 생각이 들었어. 브랜든은 내가 배고플 때마다 음식을 가져다 주는데. 내가 이걸 먹는다면, 브랜든이 배가 고플지도 몰라.

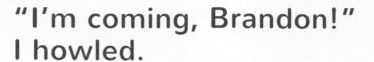

"I'm coming, Brandon!"
I howled.

"기다려, 브랜든!" 난 크게 소리쳤어.

He and his dad were way down
the street. I ran after them with
the brown bag in my mouth.

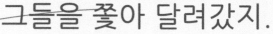

브랜든과 아빠가 도로 저 편으로 사라지고
있었어. 난 갈색 봉지를 입에 문 채로
그들을 쫓아 달려갔지.

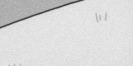

As I was passing an alleyway, I saw a cat. I hate cats! I forgot about my mission and dropped the bag.

골목을 지나갈 때쯤, 고양이 한 마리가 눈에 띄었어! 난 고양이를 싫어해! 잠시 내 할 일을 잊고 봉지를 내려놨어.

"Bark, get out of here, cat!" I barked.

"멍멍, 저리가, 이 고양이야!" 난 힘껏 짖었지.

Then I remembered Brandon's lunch. He was going to be hungry if I didn't bring him his lunch!

그 때 브랜든의 점심이 생각났어. 내가 이걸 안 가져다 주면 브랜든이 배가 고플거야!

It was hard, but I forgot about the cat. I picked up the brown bag again and started running.
쉽지는 않았지만, 난 고양이를 잊기로 했어. 다시 갈색 봉지를 물고 달리기 시작했지.

Further down the street, I stopped again.
A butcher shop!
거리를 더 내려가다가, 다시 멈추고 말았어. 정육점!

There were pieces of meat and sausages
hanging everywhere. Mmmmm...
가게 안은 온통 고기와 소시지들로 가득차 있었지.
흠…

Wait! I had to bring Brandon his lunch or he
was going to be hungry!
잠깐! 브랜든에게 점심을
가져다 주지 않으면 배가
무척 고플 텐데!

It was hard, but I forgot about the meat.
I grabbed the lunch and started running
again.

쉽진 않았지만, 고기에 대해선 생각하지
않기로 했어. 난 봉지를 들고 다시
달리기 시작했어.

I turned a corner and stopped. There was another dog wagging his tail.

골목을 돌자마자 다시 멈춰섰어. 이번엔 다른 강아지 한 마리가 꼬리를 흔들고 있었지.

"Hi, want to play?" he woofed.

"안녕, 같이 놀까?" 녀석이 물었어.

"I sure do!" I answered. "Oh, wait, I can't right now. I have to bring Brandon his lunch."

"그럼, 좋지!" 내가 답했지. "아, 잠깐, 지금은 안되겠어. 브랜든에게 점심을 가져다 줘야 하거든."

It was hard, but I forgot about playing. I grabbed the lunch and started running again.

쉽진 않았지만, 노는 건 잠시 미루기로 했지. 점심을 들고 다시 달리기 시작했어.

I could see the school—and there was Brandon with his dad! I ran as fast as I could.

이제 학교가 보이기 시작했어—그리고 브랜든과 아빠도 보였어! 난 최대한 빨리 달려갔어.

Stopping in front of Brandon, I dropped his lunch bag on the sidewalk. Just in time!

브랜든 앞에 서서, 점심이 든 봉지를 내려놨어. 딱 맞춰 왔지 뭐야!

"Look, Dad, he brought my lunch!" exclaimed Brandon.

"아빠, 이거 봐요, 강아지가 제 점심을 가져 왔어요!" 브랜든이 소리쳤어.

"Wow, he sure did. That's amazing!" said his dad. They both patted me on the head.

"우와, 정말이네. 대단한 걸!" 아빠도 말했어. 그들은 내 머리를 쓰다듬어 줬지.

Brandon was happy and so was his dad.
브랜든과 아빠는 무척 기뻐했어.

In fact, his dad was so happy that he brought me home. He gave me a bath. He gave me food!
사실, 아빠가 너무 감탄한 나머지 나를 집으로 데려갔어. 목욕도 시켜주고, 먹을 것도 주었지!

Now when Brandon and his dad go walking, I get to walk with them. And when they go home, I get to go home with them!
이젠, 브랜든과 아빠가 산책갈 때면, 나도 같이 따라가. 집으로 돌아올 때도, 역시 같이 오고 말이야!

I love my new home and my new family!
난 새 집과 새로운 가족들이 너무 좋아!

CPSIA information can be obtained
at www.ICGtesting.com
Printed in the USA
LVHW07*1425310518
579127LV00026B/371/P